THE PEOPLE ARE LIKE WOLVES TO ME

Poems by

William Taylor Jr.

ROADSIDE PRESS

Table of Contents

This book is dedicated to Bruno S.

All My Poems Are Coming True

The 21st century like a final curse
from a vengeful dying god,

this momentary flailing about
between two slabs of endless dark.

Toss aside the melancholy French novellas
and the pictures of people who have perished in the fires,

open the kitchen window and take in
whatever it is that's left to us:

the lonely noises of the city,
the stink of wasted hours,
the muffled sighs of the lost.

The poets are spent,
grasping at tired words,
disintegrating into the ether.

The books and the poems
and the paintings are all born
of plastic machines.

The empty cars drive themselves

through the dark.

People disappear,
they go clean,

become responsible
citizens and other ghosts,

dissolved into the fear
of what is coming,

leaving only bones with no one
to remember if they ever had names.

Even of This

What to do with this dull
animal fear that lives
in your blood

these brittle hours
splintering at the touch

these days ever harder
to stoke into fire

this scarecrow of failures
this one breath closer to the last
this life of useless gestures
and false portents

what to do but make a music
even of this.

Poem for the New Year

It's the first week of February
and in my neighborhood all the
Christmas trees are still up

and shimmering in the windows
of the houses and apartment buildings.

Strings of blinking lights
still tangled in the bushes,

plastic icicles hang from wooden
eaves in the afternoon sun.

Nobody's complaining,
the absurdity is a comfort.

Otherwise we'd have just another
bleak year laid out before us
much like the others,

filled with things that frighten,
things we don't want to know
or think about.

William Taylor Jr.

We imagine these silly objects
as scarecrows of sorts,

holding the future dark at bay.

Even the little artificial thing
I threw together in late December

with its gaudy tinsel
and tiny ornaments

still sits glowing
on the desk as I type.

They ask me why
I don't put it away

and I tell them it's not
hurting anything.

The People Are Like Wolves to Me

I walk the city,
its hills and alleyways,
nervous beneath the sun.
I've got the ancient and abiding sorrow of things
pulled about me like a tattered shawl,
my memories of everyone
who was ever any good
crumpled in the pockets
of my coat,
along with old letters
and pretty stones.
I see everybody's loneliness
flowing through their hairstyles
and their laundry all strung up
and swaying between buildings
like strange flags.
The people are like wolves to me,
the way they are always hungry,
the way they circle about
with shining eyes
in search of weakness.
A woman in a doorway
calls me beautiful
and asks to tell my future.

I politely decline,
telling her I know it
well enough.
We never asked for this, you know,
we were perfectly content
to bask oblivious in the void,
yet here we are caught
in the fraying net of existence
as the poems and the years
grow thin.
To be clear,
I am not demanding justice
or recompense
for what has become of us,
I am merely petitioning
that this beauty,
this terror,
this suffering through the moments
be noted in the ledgers
of the universe,
even if as a footnote.
Let it not be stricken
from the record.

Immortality

Time has it in for me like never before,
and these dreams of immortality
refuse to chase themselves.
All my half-assed and half-finished
poems are scattered about this table
in this Grant St. dive
that was once a coffeehouse
where Janis played when she first
came to San Francisco,
back in what were known
as more colorful times.
Now it's the tail end of summer
in what passes for the 21st century,
each day shorter than the last.
They're playing early Black Sabbath
and my beer tastes of pine.
The women are beautiful
beneath the North Beach sun
as they always are.
The bartender is called Lily.
She's tattooed, apathetic, and a little mean
in the way that bartenders can be.
I don't have it in me to pretend
to have much of anything to say
that I haven't bored you

with a few times over,
so I drink my beer and watch the girls
as a hair metal band reminds me
that we don't need nuthin'
but a good time.
I nod along to the
wisdom of music,
deciding immortality
is for losers
and chumps.

A Photograph I Want to Paint

The end times have found us
on a Sunday afternoon in September

as we loll about these afterthought days
simply because they're the devil
we know.

I wander the Tenderloin
and end up at Emperor Norton's

where I sit at the bar with a quiet kinship
between myself and the handful of others

staring down their drinks
as the hours slink off to die.

It's as good a church as any,

a temporary haven from the meaner things
the world would show us.

I like the big windows looking out onto Larkin St.

where men fight with bottles and knives
and nod off in sidewalk tents.

William Taylor Jr.

There's a pretty junkie girl and she
stumbles a bit, leaning
on a wall laughing a pretty
junkie laugh

like a photograph I want to paint
as everything slides into whatever.

A Pretty Scandinavian Girl was Playing the Piano

There was a party in the alley outside the North Beach bar.
A pretty Scandinavian girl was playing the piano
and singing, she was quite something.
Everybody sat at tables and drank and watched.
One by one people got up to dance—
the lady poet with the flowing scarves
the lady painter with the swirling skirts
the dude poet with the beret and some kind of little flute
and the tourists who were just passing by,
all of them up there dancing and laughing,
swinging each other around with abandon
like something from a film.
I sat there annoyed with the fact of them
being so easy with their joy,
oblivious to their imperfect bodies
as they flailed them about,
bitter that my own joy
was broken and wouldn't
let me dance in broad daylight
as the pretty Scandinavian girl banged the keys.

William Taylor Jr.

Your Stupid Heart

Hey friend, tell me
what's left

of your
stupid heart.

I want to know
what music

resides within you,

what secret joy
is yet undone,

what scrap of beauty
you've kept hidden
from the thieves.

Have you harnessed
the horror of the average day

with some new
form of laughter,

a graceful movement
of the hand?

Have you learned
to sing like fire?

Tell me as we drink this wine

and cast tomorrow
and all their dumb

and empty faces
into oblivion.

What the People Want

All the people want is the saddest song
they've ever known
playing on repeat at 3 a.m.

and someone's assurance
that their failings are predestined
and pretty in the eyes of a kind
and forgiving universe.

They just want a new drug
to make them forget everything
that's ever happened
and remember it all forever at once,

with no cancer
or hangover in the morning.

They just want directions
to the nearest fire escape,
the closest chicken exit,

a back door in the break room
somebody forgot to lock.

The people only want to live long enough
to have revenge upon the world
and then a quiet place to lay their head
as they drift off to the white noise
of the end of it all.

They just want to feel life's great fire
coursing through their blood
one last time even if it
kills them.

They want the sad music to play
all through the night

and then for the dawn
to forget their name.

Bukowski's Shoelace

The great loneliness of the world
like some perfect eternal machine.

I pace its belly
as the hours fall away.

This moment to moment
makes me nervous,

this milling about until the next
terrible thing.

This ceaseless trickling
of ordinary dooms

wearing us down like
Bukowski's shoelace

and we're not even allowed
to scream.

I drink beer in protest
and watch the people walk

along Polk Street beneath

the August sun.

They talk and laugh
as if there were still

a chance for something

and I cling to the feel of it
like a last ticket home.

The Same Poem I Always Write

I'm at the Lush Lounge on Polk St.
and I order a blood orange IPA.
Crystal the pretty bartender says,
It's a blood orange kinda day.
I affirm this truth and retire
to my table by the window
where I scratch my words
onto paper scraps
with nothing in particular to declare
other than the usual half-formed thoughts
upon the absurdity of life
and the absurdity of death
and the fact of myself
caught between the two
with my tiny mumblings
against the void.
It's the same poem I always write
but I like to think each time
with some new sound or color or gesture,
some new snapshot of continuing
that someone might see
and understand in their way.
The hours turn to ghosts
and these useless moments
come and go and we jump

from each to each like
tiny islands as they disappear
because we don't know
what else to do.
I figure if the big grey sky
cast up over the sad old buildings
has the power to break my heart
on more days than not
that's reason enough
to continue.

William Taylor Jr.

Fight Them

Honey there's no shame
in joy,

what with death
and all her henchmen

forever at our heels,

lying in wait
at every intersection.

Honey break the rotten
world in two,

scrape out
whatever's left

that could still
be any good.

It's yours as much
as anyone's.

Fight them for it.

The Face of Art

The celebrated poet died last week.

He'd written hundreds
of books across the years,

visited many countries,
gave countless readings
and speeches in little rooms.

He held court at tables in pubs
and bars throughout the land
far into the night,

declaiming the truth that evil
is powerless in the face of art,

but throughout it all

the wars didn't stop
and the downtrodden remained
as they were.

Those in charge of violence
remained oblivious to his words
and his name.

Still, at the news of his death
we marched in the streets,

we sang songs
and waved flowers
in his honor.

Later we sat drinking wine
talking of his genius

as somewhere far away
another building collapsed into fire.

How Many Summers

It seems your death has finally
caught up with me, some
two years on.

The truth of never seeing you again.

I always imagined I would
see you again.

Remember July in Santa Cruz,
say 1997,
you in that dress,

the two of us trudging up the hill
to the boardwalk,

the big sun shining down,
my backpack heavy
with wine.

Jesus Christ, I don't know
how many summers

I have left in me
but I would trade

at least a few

to have that one
back.

Why We Sing

The universe is forever
indifferent to our sorrow

and this is why we
make a music of it.

We are god-forgotten
and this is why we dance
the way we do,

why we reach for fire
and other things
that burn,

why we learn the language
of everything gone
and turn it into song.

Each day we wake
into a world already lost

and this is why we sing.

Art

I'm working at my painting,
trying capture the figure of a woman
but the hands are giving me trouble.

I've never learned to love
power or money enough
to hold much of either.

I've lost faith in the prospects
of myself and most others.

I no longer believe
there is much that
can be saved

and I've made what peace with it I can.

The world and its people are out there
doing their harm,

the future like a dark
and ill-formed beast
perched atop some building
in the distance.

I sit momentarily safe enough
behind these walls
trying to paint better hands.

Beneath the Judgment of the Sun

I'm back in Bakersfield
for the first time in years,
drunk at some tired hotel
down by the jail
and the bail bond stations.
I'm here for a wedding,
a funeral, something.
I'm wandering the streets
marveling at how people
still live and die their lonely lives
in these shabby houses by the train stations
with the dying lawns and the brown plastic
kiddie pools half filled with brackish water,
the rusted sprinklers, the dented mail boxes
with little red flags uselessly raised.
People wander the parking lots
like bitter zombies blasted
on whatever it is they could score.
Out on Chester Avenue
the pretty girls are still too young
for their clothes, their eyes,
the smiles on their faces.
The boxlike churches
all painted white, each the same,
dark birds circling above.

My parents are gone, strangers
dwell in my childhood home, the streets
overrun with gangs and neglect.
I consider my friends,
my brother and sister,
and I wonder what it is
that's kept them here.
Some of the old bars are decent enough,
quiet, dim, and unassuming,
useful still for hiding from the day.
But now I'm back out beneath
the judgment of the sun,
walking the wide and empty boulevards
lined with decomposing houses.
I note the sad stories told by objects
abandoned in the gutters,
I feel the presence of every
sad ghost, wondering if
they miss me the way
I do them.

Another Little Piece

I was drinking outside Tupelo
on Grant Avenue in North Beach.
The bartender was beautiful
and drunk as she ran outside
to tell the guy in the bigass truck
to quit honking his fucking horn.
After he flipped her off
and sped away, she asked
if I thought she'd been rude.
I said hell no, he had it coming.
She lit a cigarette and asked
what I was reading. It was
some pretentious tome
and when I spoke of it her eyes
glossed over and she told me
how she'd just finished
a biography of Janis Joplin.
She told me how she'd loved
Janis ever since she was a kid
because they shared the same energy.
She told me how when Janis first
came to San Francisco she would sing
at the bar on the corner just a few
feet from where we stood,
back when it was still the Coffee Gallery.

We talked of the history of the city
and of the neighborhood,
the literature and the music,
and at some point she ran inside
for more cigarettes and brought
me another beer. She told me
how Grant St. was the very first
road built in San Francisco
and many other things that I forget.
Her hair was gold beneath the sun
as it disappeared between the old
wooden buildings
and I wanted to disintegrate
into forever beneath her gaze.
Her cheeks glistened with quiet tears
as she spoke of Janis and her messy
tragic life, and then the sun was gone
and we were both very drunk.
She hugged me told me
I was beautiful
and I hugged her told her
she was beautiful.
When I got home I ordered
a copy of the book,
and though in the past
I never much thought about
Janis one way or another,

when I sat down and watched
the video of her singing
"Ball and Chain"
at the Monterey Pop Festival
I may have teared up a bit myself.

What Every Poem is Trying to Tell You

Over wine the famous old poet
tells me how all he can think of anymore
is the fact of his own death.

It dogs him through his waking hours
and keeps him from sleep.

I'm 20 years behind him
and already spend too many hours
contemplating the looming
eternity in which I will not exist.

It's what every poem is trying to tell you.

It's why we drink and fornicate
and go to church,

why we fall in love with apathetic bartenders
and assign meaning to the alignment of the stars.

It's why we read Dostoevsky and Camus

and travel to faraway places
with exotic buildings and food,

William Taylor Jr.

why we nod to ourselves reassuringly
when we read that 56 is the new 37

and scour the internet
for something to make us
bigger and wiser than death,

desperate for any distraction
from the coming dark

and the old poet's
haunted dreams.

Down at Turk and Taylor

You can still go to the Tenderloin
on a Saturday night and lose yourself

in the noise and the terror
of the dirty shining streets,

the life and the death
all swirling about

in the lights
and the rain.

You can evaporate into the cries
and the laughter of the broken
and the lost,

buy a poet's heart
down at Turk & Taylor
no more damaged than the next.

You can stop for a drink
in some little place

with hip hop on the jukebox
and pretty girls playing pool

where you try and get a few lines down
before they disappear,

where you try and give a voice to this,

to glean some kind of truth
from the lonely men at the bar,

imagining the right word
the right line

will open a window
into something necessary

and trick another moment from a world
that has already forgotten your name.

The Girl at the Record Store Counter

Despite what the inspirational memes would suggest,
it's more than likely things will not be okay
anytime soon.
As we wait for the eternal silence to restore its mercy
you and me and everyone we love
will be burdened with more than we can bear.
Our nightmares will come true as often as not
and we will look as old in photographs as we imagine we do.
The loneliness that haunts our bones will find no other home.
Beauty is expendable and will be first on the chopping block
when it all comes down.
The poets and the artists have not saved us,
the pretty bartender will not read your book
and the girl at the record store counter
is forever unimpressed with your choices.
Death will arrive as pointless and as certain
as an ad for something you never wanted
and couldn't afford if you did.
But music exists,
and the fire and noise of our blood.
If you're lucky enough and you work it right
you can choose a bit how your heart is broken
and that's as good a deal as anyone's gonna give you.

Mourning

Lawrence Ferlinghetti died three days ago
and since then my artist friend has wandered
the streets of North Beach with a haunted face,

his hands clasped tight behind him
like the old men of Chinatown,

with the jacket, hat, and scarf
he wears most every day, looking like something
from a painting by Toulouse-Lautrec.

When he passes City Lights he pauses
to gaze at the memorials, the bunches
of flowers strewn about the sidewalk

and solemnly kneels to read
something someone has written
on the concrete in bright pink chalk.

He stays there, motionless, his eyes
staring deep into some other place.

I'm not close enough to say for sure,
but I imagine a single tear plowing
slowly down his cheek.

When he rises he turns to me and says,
with a voice like something coming up for air,

I've been interviewed by three television crews today,
because they could sense I was in MOURNING!

He speaks the word like he means it in the purest sense
and his eyes shine with grief as he wanders off.

A part of me considers it all a bit absurd,
a performative show,

but maybe he's the only guy around
who remembers how to mourn a poet
the way a poet should be mourned,

another art all but lost
into this dark mess of everything
devouring whatever light
we try and give.

Speaker Noise

It was Bakersfield, circa 1985.
We were misfits in black,
high school and college dropouts,
jobless as often as not.
Scared of girls,
scared of boys,
scared of most everything
the world had to offer us.
We'd sleep by day
and in the afternoons we'd wander
the malls and parking lots.
Most nights I'd gather us up
in my puke-colored Datsun
and we'd stop by the 7-11
to grab a case of whatever swill
we favored at the time.
We'd end up somewhere,
most often a neighborhood park,
where we'd sit at a picnic table
with a boombox and a little suitcase
of cassette tapes.
We'd drink and smoke and listen
to our punk and our deathrock,
our jangly guitars.

We didn't talk much,
we'd argue a bit
about what to put on next,
but mostly we'd just lose ourselves
in the speaker noise.
Sometimes the cops chased us away
but mostly they left us alone.
Now and then one of us would bust out
 a mixtape we'd made.
We put a lot of time and thought
into those and I remember the one
I was most proud of. I christened it:
Shitty Bitch: A Collection of Love Songs.
It was a bunch of noisy tunes
about being dumped or passed over
because I was mad at a girl
for breaking my sullen
and misunderstood heart.
It always felt good
watching your friends nod along
to the songs you chose,
saying fuck yeah now and then
as they sipped at their beer.
It helped a bit to feel
that they understood life
and its trouble
in the same way you did.

William Taylor Jr.

You felt a little less alone
when Rollins screamed
some line that cut straight through you
with its truth,
and your buddy opens
another beer
and says, goddamn right.

What Anybody Else is Looking For

It's a warm April evening
and I'm out in North Beach
drinking drinks
and looking at the pretty people,
basking in the music and the lights.
I'm too shy to dance but it's fun to watch.
I'm sitting at a table outside of Mr. Bing's,
an aging biker chick stops
and chats with me a bit until she gets bored
and drifts off into eternity.
I didn't understand half the stuff
she was saying, but I liked her okay
and wouldn't have minded
if she'd stuck around,
but I guess I didn't have whatever it was
she was looking for.
That's a common thing, these days,
hardly anybody seems to have
what anybody else is looking for.
They call it the human condition,
I think.
Just like the rest of us,
the world's gone on too long
and no longer knows what to do
with itself.

A drunk guy steps outside to smoke.
He's overly friendly and he's asking me questions
but he doesn't have whatever it is
I'm looking for.
I shrug and turn away
and pretend to write
this poem.

The Only Path

Don't beat yourself up
too much about it, kid.

Sure, you're not everything
you thought you'd be

but that's how it is
for most of us.

All those people
you've disappointed,

they probably had it coming.

Give yourself some days of silence,
forget to hustle for a while.

Understand the universe
will forget you and everything
you have and haven't done.

Find some peace in this
and sleep, guiltlessly,

and then get up

whenever it is

you feel like
getting up

and do something beautiful
and useless,

because that's the only
path to grace.

Out on Market Street There's a Guy

Out on Market Street there's a guy
with a loudspeaker and he's talking
about my relationship with Jesus,

he says my good works aren't enough
and if I really wanna get saved
I need to open my heart
and get straight with the Lord.

There's another guy with a sign that tells me
how the government has rays
up there in the sky

all set to shoot down
straight into my brain
when I least expect.

I guess it's good to have people
to enlighten me on such matters
but I can't get too worked up about it all.

I don't think there's much I can do about the rays
and I'm concerned with more immediate things

like how Old Navy is out of my size
of the only jeans I really like

and the place where I go to buy affordable
footwear has closed down.

If Jesus really cares about the little guy
he should think more about these kinds of things

and if he really wants to have a conversation
I'm happy to open my heart
over a handful of beers but I got
no time for his sidewalk lackeys.

See, I don't need an eternity of bliss
just a good pair of skinny black jeans
so I can look good beneath the rays.

The Fact of Her

In San Francisco
at any given moment
there is a girl
in North Beach
on Grant St.
wearing a long
and fashionable coat.
She's got raven black hair
tumbling down
her shoulders
a cup of wine
in one hand
maybe a cigarette
in the other,
looking
like something
from an old
French film.
She's swaying
on the sidewalk
to music from a bar
or a man playing
guitar on a corner.
Maybe she knows
you're watching,

maybe she doesn't
but the thing is
the simple fact of her
makes all the rest of it
worth suffering
through.

The Famous Dead Poet's House

I went to the famous dead poet's house
on a Thursday afternoon
because I am paid to do such things.
The famous dead poet had been dead
a few years when the offspring
were notified that the home
had been sold and the dead poet's things
were to be cleared out within the week.
I was there to dig through the mess of it
with the hope of finding something
that could be auctioned off
for big money.
The famous dead poet's house
was a disappointment to me,
a generic thing in an upscale
San Francisco neighborhood,
nothing befitting a famous dead poet.
When I arrived the famous dead poet's
daughter met me outside.
She was arguing on her phone
with someone about one of the in-laws,
saying she didn't want him around
picking through all the stuff.
If that fucker comes by, she said, *I'm bailing.*
She ended the call and told me

not to talk to the fucker if he came by
and then took me down to an oppressively
hot and dimly lit garage where
the famous dead poet's books
sat dusty upon plastic shelves
and left me there to pick through them
in search of undiscovered treasure.
It was an unexceptional library,
ordinary editions of all the books
you would expect. Mostly poetry
by other dead poets, the usual
works of literature and philosophy
and a smattering of new age junk.
I found a first edition of Ginsberg's
collected poems inscribed by him
to the famous dead poet.
I showed it to the famous dead poet's kid
and her eyes lit up as she asked me
what it was worth. I told her what
it was worth and her eyes went dim again
as she set it back upon the shelf.
I scanned the books a while more
until I had to tell her there was
nothing else worth mentioning.
She pointed to a pile of boxes
which she claimed held things of a more
personal nature and hovered about as I

shuffled through random indecipherable
papers, scribbled notes for classes
and workshops, things of mild interest
and little value. I grew weary of the sad
boxes and their sad contents and I gave
the famous dead poet's kid my card
and told her to call if she discovered anything
of interest I may have overlooked.
She took it with a disappointed gaze,
acknowledging my failure.
I trudged sweaty up the hard stone stairs
out of the dark and the heat and the sad old books,
the boxes of dust and death and disappointment
and emerged beneath the afternoon sun
feeling better straight away.

The Broken Hearts of Larkin St.

It's all just drinking wine and waiting
for the next terrible thing to arrive,

harboring visions of something like mercy
despite the universe having no history of such.

The slow and tedious decay of things
hums along in time with the tune
of how it is we became this way.

Shuffling through the hours
along the path of least resistance

with eyes like children
in old photographs,

hearts of lukewarm ash,

desperate for something to cram in our blood
stronger than religion or drugs.

It's the future now and driverless cars
drift like ghost machines in the night

and for $12.99 a month

the chatbots will send us nudes
and tell us that our poems are pretty

but there's nothing for the broken hearts of Larkin St.

where the driverless wheelchairs
lay on their sides where they fell.

Still I like to imagine there's a chance
that the lost and the dead and the forgotten

will some day rise up with the fury
of every wasted year

and tear down the world and everything,
stoke the loneliness at the heart of it

into a fire so great that god might see
and finally be ashamed.

Shaking it Off

Friends, let's celebrate this moment
simply because it's here and will not
be so again.

It's a bright afternoon in San Francisco.

I'm in Chinatown and they're playing
the Velvet Underground at Mr. Bing's.

Death wouldn't dare to show
its face around here, not today.

The dark got ahold of me early on
but sometimes I can still
shake it off a bit

with another half-ass poem,
another golden beer beneath
a golden sun

as the love and the light
slip through the cracks
of the void as best they can.

Let me have this

as the people drink
and laugh and smoke,

and the old love songs play
and play like nothing
could end.

In Search of It

I'm at the de Young Museum in San Francisco
viewing the works of Tamara de Lempicka,
her beautiful Art Deco women and men,

pressing myself close to the paintings,
studying the shapes and colors,
trying to glean their secrets.

The people have failed me,
the government has failed me,
I have failed myself.

All of which is commonplace,

but I've grown bitter with hope
forever tricking me
into mucking through it all
just to reach the next rotten thing.

Yet here I am in search of it,
wandering the rooms and hallways
gazing upon the creations of the dead,

wondering if Tamara de Lempicka can save me
when nothing else has,

wondering if the others crowded about me,
the tourists, the old men, the young girls
all shuffling and staring, are wondering the same.

I wonder if this glass of wine in the museum garden
in tandem with the chilly sunlight and the women
in their fashionable coats will have the power
to pull me back from the edge of things?

Will writing it down in my little red book bring some justice?
Will translating it to my laptop and sending it to a journal
where it will be read by 7 people finally beat back the dark?

Will printing it out and reading it aloud
in a North Beach bar where it will be lost
amidst the noise and laughter set things right
within me when all else has failed?

It hasn't so far,
but maybe it has.

Something as Decent

I am once more drunk
in the afternoon.

Call it my little bit of
raging against

the machine,

the dying of the light,

and the general
dreariness of things.

I'm drinking wine
at a fashionable
Polk St. bar.

The people are pretty
and dull,

their chatter
is a kind of music,

and you,

if these words have
somehow found you,

I hope you're okay.

Whoever,
wherever,
whenever
you are,

I hope that something good
still exists for you.

I hope there is still music,

a distant woman's laughter,

or at least something
as decent

as being drunk
in the afternoon.

A Poem or Something

I like hanging out in North Beach
and finding a quiet place
to sit and drink

while pondering the world and maybe
wrestling a poem or something
from the sorry mess of it.

Sometimes it's hard, mostly
because of the poets.

The poets are everywhere—
the bars and the cafes,
the liquor stores and the street corners.

And the poets like to talk.
Hardly anybody likes to talk
the way the North Beach poets like to talk,

which can be an issue
if you're trying to write a poem.

I'm currently hiding in a wine bar that plays
heavy metal records at a loud volume.

The People Are Like Wolves to Me

The poets tend to stay away from here.

If I'm lucky I'll have a bit of time before
one of them sees me though the window
and wants to buy me a beer or borrow 5 dollars,

time enough to scratch out a skeleton
of this thing that sits inside me
refusing me peace until I grant it
some semblance of a life outside.

I decide this will have to do for now.

I suck down my drink
and head back into the night,

in search of something I cannot name,
and some poets who will listen to me
talk about it.

A Song For Alleys

She told me she liked alleys.

I am the same and offer up
this song to those sanctuaries
of dirt and concrete,

recognized by all decent beings
as places of temporary refuge,

havens from the poisoned claws
of the world so hungry
to do us harm.

The good people stride
well-lit streets on their way
to places dumb with purpose
and fortune,

people with no use for alleys.

They turn their gaze to brighter things
and don't think to pause to ask us

exactly what it is we're doing here,
in this space between the structures,

continuing on to their own whatevers.

Shame won't show its face here,
the sun remains indifferent.

The moon will not judge our misjudgments,
our desperate arms, our busted kisses.

The pavement knows our kind.

Regret has business elsewhere
and even the cops

leave us alone
for a while.

Poem Written While Getting a Decent Buzz Before Going to the Record Store

I'm still a sucker for the gorgeous absurdity
of the people walking along Haight St.
beneath the old San Francisco sky,
buying records and tacos and whiskey-ginger ales,
the impossible beauty of a young woman
studying the menu at a sidewalk table,
the tour busses and the big-eyed
street kids still searching for the summer of love.
I drink beer outside Murio's and imagine myself
the Walt Whitman of the end times.
The biker chick bartender is pleasantly indifferent
and a gin-drinking woman tries to engage me in conversation.
She wants to tell me about how everything
was different in the 1970s,
how this building used to be another building
and how this jukebox used to be a different jukebox
with different songs
but I take my drink outside to my plastic table
where I might better write about my loneliness.
A large man drinking many whiskeys
as he talks on his phone asks me what I do.
I tell him something vague
and he tells me I look like a star,
he tells me he's in the music industry.

He wants to tell me stories
about the people and things he's done
but I shake his hand and tell him
I have to catch a bus.
He spills whiskey on his shirt and tie
as he laughs and waves me away.
A few blocks away a man in a dirty dinosaur outfit
asks me for change as the punk kids sneer
and the sidewalk Deadheads grin and take another hit,
immune to death and other machinations of the man,
all of us caught here together
in the poisonous glory of whatever
the hell this is, our dumbass hearts
breaking eternally for nothing in particular
and everything at once.

You're Not Wilfred Owen

You're not Wilfred Owen, we don't need another poem
reminding us how war is an unkind thing,
and how the death of children is something
civilized folk should have no truck with.

War and its lackeys wipe their asses with poetry
and dying children have no interest in such things.

What we could really use are poems reminding us to be
ashamed
of how we daily throw away our lives at the whims
of the dull and the servile.

Give us not your poems workshopped into bland competence,
rendered useless and sterile, dead upon the vine,

poems of virtue by the virtuous,
pristine of craft but lacking heart,

poems as useless
as bags of tissue paper in the rain,

poems that couldn't get themselves arrested.

The People Are Like Wolves to Me

Give us poems as broken and as frightened
and as unrepentant as our problematic souls,

imperfect poems with imperfect voices,
demanding to exist without permission of the community.

Give us poems reminding us it is worthwhile to be alive
despite the evidence suggesting otherwise.

Get outta town with your poems born only
to chase down the lowest common
denominator of a mediocre heart.

Give us poems that speak
in the ancient language of fire,
because death is on our ass

and the whole world's trying to sell us
their empty words even though
we've already paid.

Another Fucking Poem about Drinking at Vesuvio
for Hugh Blanton

The North Beach poets sit at the bar
and drink at all hours
in their funny hats and coats,
as if there were nothing else in the world
that ever needed doing.

The Anarchist girl sits alone
drinking dark beer and reading a book
about the rise of techno fascism.

And me, I'm forever on the run
from death and her yes men,

a glass of wine at my favorite
table in the back corner of the balcony
beneath the painting of the bare breasted woman.

I tear my little poems from the jagged
teeth of the dark the best I am able

as the pretty girls in Kerouac Alley
sit at little round tables smoking
cigarettes and drinking beer.

The People Are Like Wolves to Me

I gaze down upon them
and pretend I am in Paris.

I've never been to Paris
and It's looking like I might
not ever make it,
even though I'd like to.

Some people do things like go to Paris
and others muddle through life
one moment to the next

and I figure that's just the way
it is and there's no sense getting
upset.

There's still some poetry to be mined here
despite what the years have taken.

I lean back and bask in the feel of it,
thinking of all those suckers in Paris
who will never get the chance.

The People Who've Been to Hell and Back

The people who've been to hell and back,
you know it right away,

even if they're too polite
to talk about it.

You can hear it in their voices
and smell it on their jackets.

There's a look in their eyes
that makes you nervous.

Get a few drinks in them
and they'll loosen up a bit,
they'll tell you

how Dante only saw the guest rooms
and never set foot in the
dirty parts of town.

The people who've been to hell and back
will not suffer bad poetry
or good intentions.

They have great fashion sense
and the best record collections.

They find the beauty and the terror
in all the places you never thought to look.

They'll tell you hell is just like
the most terrible things you've dreamed
only you don't wake up.

They can see all your secrets as if
they were branded in light
upon your skin.

They could tell you your fate
like a cheap vaudeville trick,

reveal your final destination
in great and unwarranted detail,

but by the time they got around to it
you'd be already there.

The Edge of It

Each day she wakes and throws herself
straight into the fire of the world,

the dark and terrible heart of it,

embracing the chaos,

taking its laughter
as her own.

She says its the only way
she knows to live.

I follow as far as I am able

and then wait here
at the edge of it,

holding her things.

The Only Time God Exists

There's that thing in your eyes
I catch now and then
that says we're broken
in the same way,
and these days the only time god
exists is when we're finally
drunk enough to kiss.
Your laughter in the dark
like a city on fire,
a riot at the end of the world,
like escaping through barbed wire
back into the sun,
burning with the righteous
fury of the damned.
It makes me want to write love poems
now that it's too late for love poems,
because that's the only time they're real.

Carnival

Understand that every scrap of light
you peel from the dark,
in whatever fashion you can afford,
is a victory worth noting.
It's like being at the county fair
and winning the skull and crossbones ring,
the Led Zeppelin mirror,
the Farrah Fawcett poster,
and the oversized stuffed panda bear
that you'll give to the girl you like
in physical science class,
because you somehow managed
to pop enough balloons
or get enough balls in the holes
or you banged the thing hard enough
with the giant mallet,
even when chance,
god, and the drunken
carnival barker
were all dead
against you.

Even Now

Even though this afterthought century
has been cast off and abandoned
on the scrapheap of eternity,

and all the clever and beautiful things
have been written and said,

even though there's not much left to do
but hold it all together long enough
to die,

you can still wander these
San Francisco streets

a little bit drunk,

stumbling through the fog
and the pretty gray

with no destination
in mind,

adrift with the other ghosts,

singing like
you had a reason.

William Taylor Jr.

And the Sound of the Rain

Even the most beautiful things
come to such ignoble ends

and nothing you love stays with you
long enough to do any good.

It's rough to be sure
but you learn to deal with it
or you don't get very far.

Me, I stick around
because I like the feel of the sun
and the sound of the rain

and on better days I think

that maybe there's another
poem left in me

and could be there's still a chance

she'll brush my hand
again in the dark

even if it's just on accident.

Publication Notes

Some of the poems in this collection have appeared in the following publications: *As It Ought To Be, Chiron Review, Fevers of the Mind, Gorko Gazette, Hobo Camp Review, Horror Sleaze Trash, Misfit Magazine, One Art, Pixelated Shroud, Rusty Truck, San Pedro River Review, Thin Slice of Anxiety, Trailer Park Quarterly*

William Taylor Jr. lives and writes in San Francisco. He is the author of numerous books of poetry, and a volume of fiction. His work has been published widely in journals across the globe, including *Rattle, The New York Quarterly,* and *The Chiron Review.* He was a recipient of the 2013 Kathy Acker Award, and edited *Cocky Moon: Selected Poems of Jack Micheline* (Zeitgeist Press, 2014). *A Room Above A Convenience Store,* (Roadside Press) was his latest collection of poetry.

MORE ROADSIDE PRESS TITLES

MORE ROADSIDE PRESS TITLES

MORE ROADSIDE PRESS TITLES

www.ingramcontent.com/pod-product-compliance
Lightning Source LLC
Chambersburg PA
CBHW021128130626
46554CB00002B/920